Farmyard Tales Flip Books
The Naughty Sheep

Heather Amery

Illustrated by Stephen Cartwright

Language consultant: Betty Root
Series editor: Jenny Tyler

There is a little yellow duck to find on every page.

This is Apple Tree Farm.

This is Mrs. Boot, the farmer. She has two children, called Poppy and Sam, and a dog called Rusty.

On the farm there are seven sheep.

The sheep live in a big field with a fence around it.
One sheep has a black eye. She is called Woolly.

Woolly is bored.

Woolly stops eating and looks over the fence.
"Grass," she says, "nothing but grass. Boring."

Woolly runs out of the gate.

She runs out of the field into the farmyard. Then she runs through another gate into a garden.

Woolly sees lots to eat in the garden.

She tastes some of the flowers. "Very good,"
she says, "and much prettier than grass."

Can you see where Woolly walked?

She walks around the garden, eating lots of the flowers. "I like flowers," she says.

Mrs. Boot sees Woolly in the garden.

"What are you doing in my garden?" she shouts.
"You've eaten my flowers, you naughty sheep."

Mrs. Boot is very cross.

"It's the Show today," she says. "I was going to pick my best flowers for it. Just look at them."

It is time for the Show.

"Come on," says Poppy. "We must go now. The
Show starts soon. It's only just down the road."

They all walk down the road.

Woolly watches them go. She chews her
flower and thinks, "I'd like to go to the Show."

Woolly goes to the Show.

Woolly runs down the road. Soon she comes to a big field with lots of people in it.

Woolly goes into the ring.

She pushes past the people and into the field.
She stops by a man in a white coat.

Mrs. Boot finds her.

"What are you doing here, Woolly?" says Mrs. Boot.
"She has just won a prize," says the man.

Woolly is the winner.

"This cup is for the best sheep," says the man.
"Oh, that's lovely. Thank you," says Mrs. Boot.

It is time to go home.

"Come on, Woolly," says Mrs. Boot. "We'll take you
back to your field, you naughty, clever sheep."

They all climb out of the ditch.

"We all need a good bath," says Mrs. Boot.
"Rusty found Curly. Clever dog," says Sam.

Now everyone is very muddy.

Sam tries to catch Curly but he falls into the mud.
Mrs. Boot grabs Curly and climbs out of the ditch.

Curly is very muddy.

Mrs. Boot picks Curly up but he struggles. Then he slips back into the mud with a splash.

"We'll have to lift him out."

"I'll get into the ditch," says Mrs. Boot. "I'm coming too," says Poppy. "And me," says Sam.

"Rusty has found Curly."

They all look in the ditch. Curly has slipped down into the mud and can't climb out.

"Why is Rusty barking?"

Rusty is standing by a ditch. He barks and barks.
"He's trying to tell us something," says Poppy.

"Perhaps he's in the garden."

They look for Curly in the garden, but he is not there. "We'll never find him," says Sam.

"Maybe he's eating the cows' food."

But Curly is not with the cows. "Don't worry,"
says Mrs. Boot. "We'll soon find him."

"That's not Curly."

"It's only a piece of rope," says Mrs. Boot. "Not Curly's tail." "Where can he be?" says Poppy.

"There he is, in the barn."

"He's in the barn," says Sam. "I can just see his tail." They all run into the barn to catch Curly.

"Where are you, Curly?"

Poppy and Sam call to Curly. "Let's look in the hen run," says Mrs. Boot. But Curly is not there.

She calls Poppy and Sam.

"Curly's gone," she says. "I need your help to find him."

Mrs. Boot feeds the pigs every morning.

She takes them two big buckets of food.
But where is Curly? He is not in the pen.

Mrs. Boot has six pigs.

There is a mother pig and five baby pigs.
The smallest pig is called Curly. They live in a pen.

This is Apple Tree Farm.

This is Mrs. Boot, the farmer. She has two children, called Poppy and Sam, and a dog called Rusty.

Farmyard Tales Flip Books

Pig gets Lost

Heather Amery

Illustrated by Stephen Cartwright

Language consultant: Betty Root
Series editor: Jenny Tyler

There is a little yellow duck to find on every page.